TEILHARD AND WOMANHOOD

TEILHARD
and
WOMANHOOD

by

André A. Devaux

Translated by

Paul Joseph Oligny, O.F.M.
and
Michael D. Meilach, O.F.M.

PAULIST PRESS DEUS BOOKS
New York, N. Y.   Glen Rock, N. J.
Amsterdam   Toronto   London

A Deus Books Edition of Paulist Press, originally published
under the title *Teilhard et la vocation de la femme* by
Editions Universitaires, Paris, France.

IMPRIMI POTEST:
Rev. Cronan Kelly, O.F.M.
Vicar of the Minister Provincial

NIHIL OBSTAT:
Rev. James J. O'Connor
Censor Librorum

IMPRIMATUR:
✠ Leo A. Pursley, D.D.
Bishop of Fort Wayne-South Bend

May 14, 1968

The Nihil Obstat and Imprimatur are official declarations
that a book or pamphlet is free of doctrinal or moral error.
No implication is contained therein that those who have
granted the Nihil Obstat and Imprimatur agree with the con-
tents, opinions or statements expressed.

Library of Congress
Catalog Card Number: 68-31259

Published by Paulist Press
Editorial Office: 304 W. 58th St., N.Y., N.Y. 10019
Business Office: Glen Rock, New Jersey 07452

Printed and bound in the
United States of America

Contents

I
Love and Union

I also asked our Lord, through her whom he willed to place above the world and the Church like a perpetual dawn, that woman become among us what she ought to be for the perfecting and salvation of the human soul (Genèse d'une Pensée, p. 150).

When Father Teilhard, according to the usual bent of his mind, envisioned the possibilities offered to the man of tomorrow, two closely related themes kept coming back to him: the theme of *love* as an affective cosmic energy, present everywhere and endowed with an "explosive" power capable of transfiguring the world, and the theme of *union* which welds beings to each other, sometimes in slavery, sometimes in emancipation.

A "savage force" in its overpowering expansiveness, love is "the most universal, the most formidable, and the most mysterious of cosmic energies, immense, ubiquitous, and always un-

3

subdued," for the history of the evolution of the Universe is intermingled with the history of the evolution of love: *evolution is amorization*. This "primitive and universal psychic energy" was already, in the eyes of Teilhard the geo-biologist, the force which intervenes in the most elementary stages of life when the latter is scarcely individualized in order to make possible the diverse forms of molecular grouping: chemical reactions, primitive reflexes, and tropisms would be the humble manifestations of this primordial love.

Then, as we ascend the scale of living creatures, the energy of love tends to become intensified and concentrated in the reproductive function. Finally, on the level of hominization, the violence inherent in the amorizing, cosmic force multiplies its unrealized capabilities. Certainly, the reproductive instinct preserves its vigor, but under the control of reflection it lends itself to disciplines and refinement. And in particular, this instinct no longer exhausts all the resources of love in which the spiritual aspect has become preponderant and serves to promote an indefinite growth: "Since, in the Universe that has become thinking, everything in the end moves in and toward the Personal, it is necessarily love, a kind of love which forms and will more and more form, in the pure state, the stuff of human energy."

There is no proportion between love as it manifests itself before the appearance of the "phenomenon of man," and love as it can become after the decisive step of *hominization*, because then, to borrow a metaphor from optics, the spectrum of its warm and penetrating light has become marvellously enriched. "With man it is no longer only the isolated and occasional attraction in view of material fecundity" that makes up the all of love, it is "an unlimited and restless possibility of contact through the spirit much more than through the body; infinitely numerous and subtle antennae which seek each other out among the delicate nuances of the soul; the attraction of growing sensitivity and reciprocal fulfillment, where preoccupation with saving the species dissolves in the vaster ecstasy of two consummating a World."

The vast movement of noogenesis is marked by a dialectical interplay of reflection and amorization. The former is "a phenomenon of individual supercentration leading the corpuscular consciousness to return upon itself and emerge in the form of thought," and the latter is the essential complement of the "great cosmic event of reflection."

Now, the union which results from this drive toward amorization being realized in the world can come about in two ways which Teilhard always clearly distinguishes: the union of *dissolution* and the union of *differentiation*. Rather than a real union, the first is an absorption in which the element is assimilated in the all, like salt dissolving in the sea. Such a "unification of coercion" opens the way to sheer totalitarianism and Teilhard rejects it unequivocally. Entirely different is the authentic union which, far from destroying the differences, exalts the originality of each of the elements which it brings together "center to center."

It is a matter, then, of a "unification by un-animity" which attests how mutilating the ego-istic closing of self is. On the contrary, "the effect of the gift we make of our being, far from threatening our ego, must be its fulfillment." Love is the creator of personality: "true union does not destroy the elements it brings together; by reciprocal fecundation and adaptation, it gives them a renewal of vitality."

In 1939, before the alarming spread of fas-cism, Teilhard very clearly discerned that the alternative with which humanity was faced was one between stifling totalitarianism and liberat-ing personalism. Just at this time Teilhard wrote *La grande Option*, in which he pointed out how "love that draws those who love each other closer together without confounding them makes them find an exaltation in this mutual contact capable, a hundred times better than any solitary pride, of raising up the most powerful and creative originalities from their very depths."

Now, progress in union makes us apt for a new degree of both association and differentiation. "In order to group themselves 'centrically,' the human particles, however compressed they are, must finally love each other (love each other all at the same time and all together)," for, "by nature (or even, we might say, by definition) sympathy is the only energy capable of bringing beings together center to center (which, incidentally, is the only way of ultra-personalizing them)."

Ever onward is the key formula of all Teilhardian thought, just as it was the ideal to which Teilhard remained faithful throughout his life. In this regard, we must not fail to call attention to a striking resemblance between the program of Father Teilhard and that of St. Francis de Sales who wrote: "Man is the perfection of love, and that is why the love of God is the end, the perfection, and intelligence of the Universe."

II
WOMAN
The Unitive Force

The scientific team and the conjugal couple give, according to Teilhard, the best illustration of unstinting union achieved through cooperative effort. In this unifying endeavor, the feminine dimension of humanity plays an outstanding role, since "by nature, woman is the unitive force." Teilhard, in fact, stressed that the relative perfection already attained by mankind entails a grave risk, that of becoming complacent in a self-satisfied independence which stifles all further effort. And woman is ideally suited to cope with this risk of proud isolation, inasmuch as she is a call to forward movement and an invitation to transcendence: "Even after achieving insight into himself through reflection, primordial man would remain unfulfilled were it not for the stimulating encounter with the other sex, in which he experiences a truly personal, centric attraction."

Face to face with woman, man understands that "the complete human molecule is a more complex synthesis and therefore a more spiritualized being than the individual person. It is a duality comprising both something masculine and something feminine." The complete human being is realized in the dyad in which the masculine and the feminine are harmonized. In a very moving autobiographical text, Teilhard does not hesitate to proclaim: "No man can do without woman any more than he can do without light, oxygen or vitamins—the evidence for this is more compelling every day."

Without any doubt, he owed this certitude, first of all, to the memories of his childhood and youth which were spent with a mother whom he admired and tenderly loved. This filial love, permeated with veneration, burst into this cry at the news (in 1936) of his mother's death: "Dear and holy mother, to whom I owe the best part of my soul." What did he mean by "the best part of his soul"? Very probably, his vocation to the priesthood and to science. Being a woman of ardent piety and of an absolute faith, Teilhard's mother transmitted to him in particular a deep devotion to the Sacred Heart of Jesus which caused him to write in a letter in 1917 to his cousin Marguerite Teillard-Chambon: "The Heart of our Lord is truly something unspeakably beautiful and satisfying. It exhausts all reality and answers all the soul's needs," [1] and later on, in litanies he himself wrote down on the back of a picture of the Sacred Heart, we find: "Heart of the heart of the World . . . Quickening of Christ . . . Taste of the World . . . Essence of all energy . . . Source and Seat of all reflection."

The intimate certitude of God's personal reality became stabilized forever in Teilhard, thanks to his mother's radiant faith: "For me as well as for her, the God of my mother was above all the Word incarnate . . . All I needed was a spark to enkindle in me the fire of his love. Now this spark unquestionably came from my mother—from the Christian mystical flame which she lighted and which illumined my soul as a child . . . Thanks to a kind of habit which goes back as far as I can remember, I have never, at any moment of my life, experienced the least difficulty in speaking to God as to a supreme Someone."

But he also felt that his first incitements to scientific research and to an optimistic vision of the Universe were also due to the influence of his mother as well as to the solid instruction given him by his father, an erudite, country gentleman. Teilhard also mentioned the indel-

[1] Cf. *The Making of a Mind*, p. 192.

ible impression caused by a simple remark his mother made one day when as a child he watched a lock of hair quickly disappear in a flame: "Console yourself, Pierre, things are not completely lost. They change, they are transformed." [2] Teilhard was initiated, in purity, to the power of woman by the witness of a mother without weakness and beyond reproach.

Later on, strong feminine friendships marked the course of the priest's life, and it was assuredly a very rich personal experience which led him to write that "no access to spiritual maturity and fullness is possible without some 'sentimental' influence which increases the sensitivity of man's mind and excites, at least initially, his power to love." Pierre Teilhard enjoyed the company of intelligent women who were inspired by an ideal, and his feminine friendships, as Claude Cuénot has remarked, played a catalytic and eminently positive role in his life.

The following autobiographical confession must be taken literally: "Since I began to come out of my sleep and began to express myself to myself, everything has developed in me under the gaze and influence of women." But it seems premature to us to want to write the history of

[2] Cf. *Présence de P. Teilhard de Chardin*, Ed. Universitaires, p. 15.

these friendships which have certainly justified "the general homage" which Teilhard said came "from the deepest strata of (his) being, toward those whose warmth and charm (had) passed drop by drop into the blood of (his) most cherished ideas." On the other hand, there is no indiscretion in bringing out the aspects which reveal his discovery of the feminine within his own family, thanks to his sisters, Francoise and Marguerite-Marie, and especially to his cousin Marguerite Teillard-Chambon. It was in their presence that he became more keenly aware of the inspirational power of femininity.

Francoise, his older sister (Sister Marie-Albéric du Sacré Coeur) was a Little Sister of the Poor in China where she died in 1911. With her Pierre Teilhard knew spiritual understanding, although he did not fail to note the differences between their approaches to life: "She followed a road where the realities of this World were much more obliterated or transcended than was the case with me." Their basic accord was built on two infinitely nourishing certitudes: the reality of God in human life and the strong joy which is born of the "anticipated possession of God" in this World.

He surely felt closer to Marguerite-Marie, who was seriously crippled with a crucifying immobility, a woman of indomitable courage whose actual experience is condensed in a book with a very Teilhardian title: *The Spiritual Energy of Suffering*. Teilhard wrote a stirring preface for this book in which he compared the destiny of his sick sister to his own: "While I, dedicated to the positive forces of the Universe, was roaming continents and seas, you, immobile, stretched out, silently transformed in the depths of your soul the worst shadows of the world into light." Toward the end, he asked this question which well expresses his thoughts on the value of suffering: "In the eyes of the Creator, tell me which one of us will have the better part?" For Teilhard, joy and suffering are "two contrary" but equally important "energies" which accumulate "in immense quantities" in the World and remain, alas! "for the most part, unused."

Marguerite-Marie died August 17, 1936. Teilhard's sorrow was great: "Her passing creates around me a kind of universal solitude, affecting all the elements of an interior World which I had slowly built up around her." For a man who was anguished by the question as to whether his message would be accepted and his vision communicated, what comfort to feel understood in the depths of one's being to be able "to think together"! Teilhard tells us in one of his letters where he evokes the memory of his dear sister: "She and I were of one mind as regards spiritual action and the interior life." The friendships of Pierre Teilhard and of his sisters were built in the depth of the soul and on the heights of spiritual communion: the feminine, then, revealed itself to him with all its exceptional aptitude for renunciation.

Closer to his spirit and to his heart was certainly his cousin Marguerite Teillard-Chambon, to whom he wrote letters during World War I. In these the genius of Teilhard expressed itself freely, at a time when his most decisive intuitions were "crystalizing." Between the two correspondents the richest dialogue began and Teilhard let his gratitude pour out in eloquent formulas: "I thank God for having you"; "once again"—this is from a letter dated November 13, 1918, the day after the Armistice—"we have experienced things together."

Speaking of this exceptional friendship, Teilhard could say that it was "like a musical note which lent a certain harmony to our entire lives." Why was this constant interchange of ideas with a woman of great intellectual breadth so precious to him? First of all, because Marguerite Teillard-Chambon was an intelligent woman who enabled Teilhard to "exteriorize himself," as he himself freely admitted, and this enabled him to test the ideas that were then germinating so vigorously in him and to clarify his vocation for himself. Secondly, because she was a strong woman who, thanks to her "attentive human sympathy" helped him regain his courage in times of anxiety: "There are always times when a person cannot stand alone." Finally, and perhaps especially, because she was a generous woman in whom Teilhard could always confide what was burdening his heart, sure that he would be rightly understood: "I will certainly need you very much," he wrote on Feb. 12, 1919, "in order to confide in you what I feel and what I am doing." Such was the exalted significance of this beautiful friendship: a luminous communication between two equally exacting consciences.

But Teilhard was aware of the dangers that surround every friendship between a man and woman; he was careful, therefore, to see to it that this friendship did not degenerate into "mutual complacency"—"lost energy and love." This was an abiding concern of his: the possible waste of love as a concentrated force in the Universe. Teilhard experienced, in the privileged case of his friendship with his cousin, that a promising relationship between a man and a woman can endure and deepen only if it is paralleled by a higher relationship uniting both parties to a third, transcendent term, Christ himself, the Center of all and at the same time the focal point of universal aspiration: "The more man is man, the more will he feel the need of dedicating himself to one greater than himself."

From this conviction welled up a prayer which we find in a letter he wrote in 1917: "May our Lord help us to make our friendship such that it may be entirely a force leading to him!" Progress in a "useful friendship" is conditioned by a common will of convergence toward a higher pole capable of transforming the primitive *dyad*, made of the coming together of the masculine and the feminine, into a *triad* where the divine crowns the united terms.

III
Love and Sexuality

A similar metamorphosis is at the heart of human love when it attains the fullness of its possibilities and totally consummates the unity toward which the lovers tend. Teilhard could speak of human love both as a psychologist and as a Christian. He was sure that it is *in* and *through* love that the "individual can develop completely." The love that makes an authentic couple of a man and woman effects that "center to center" unification, "in one vision or common passion," which altogether frees and personalizes the two beings who are united to each other.

The law that "the specific effect of love is to foster the individual's development even as it joins him to another" is verified here more clearly than anywhere else. The gift of self to the other contains the possibility of limitless enrichment, and it is by "losing" oneself in the other that one can find oneself most completely. In human love, this gift concerns the totality of the human

subject and the carnal has its share which Teilhard is careful to recognize.

The power of the sexual urge could not fail to
engage the attention of the integral phenome-
nologist: Teilhard affirms that "the mutual attraction of the sexes is so fundamental a fact
that every explanation (biological, philosophi-
cal or religious) of the World that would not
end in finding an *essential* place in its structure
is virtually condemned."

In his vision of a World in genesis through
progress in creative union, Teilhard has no difficulty in integrating a conception of sexuality
which makes of the latter a means not only of
conserving the species but especially of bringing about "the necessary synthesis of the two
principles, masculine and feminine, in the build-
ing up of the human personality." Physical
union, in fact, draws its value from the fact that
it can play an important role in that psychic
and moral "mutual completion" to which total
love must aspire: "At what moment, in fact, do
the two lovers attain the most complete possession of themselves if not when they say they
are lost in each other?"

Certainly, the procreative act preserves its
primordial importance in our present world of
becoming, but that act tends to diminish in importance as greater emphasis comes to be

placed on the mutual fulfillment of the spouses in the plenitude of conjugal harmony: "The man and the woman exist for the child—now and for a long time, as long as terrestrial life has not reached maturity. But man and woman exist for each other, more and more fully as time passes, and forever."

Teilhard, therefore, casts no suspicion on the carnal as such. This is only to be expected in the case of a thinker who places so much emphasis on the unity of matter and spirit: "The most vivid of tangible realities is the Flesh. And for Man, Flesh is the Woman." The sexual encounter is "fulfilling" to the extent to which love utilizes the carnal union to reach a more profound and spiritual communion.

Life in Teilhardian phenomenology has a twofold finality: to propagate itself by reproduction, but also and especially to gather together the forces of personalization. The body is therefore only an instrument, a means of mediation between spirits: it is a means and must be treated as such. On the contrary, "the carnal man who tries to attain the object of his passion otherwise than by pursuing the evolution of his own being, that is to say, without trying to form a kind of *new*, richer and higher, *soul* by the union of two living beings; the carnal man, in his refusal to advance, sets up a hopeless obstacle to true union: each new occasion of material pleasure removes him that much further from his genuine love." The ideal of loving union is entirely different; it is summarized in that beautiful maxim of Maurice Blondel: "United in body to form but one soul, united in soul to form but one body."

In his understanding of the role of the flesh, there stands out once again Teilhard's central thesis of *Materia Matrix*—of matter as the womb of the Spirit. Father Teilhard gave a very enlightening explanation of this in a letter to Madame Maryse Choisy: "We do not attain spirit by abandoning Matter—nor do we find spirit incomprehensibly juxtaposed with Matter, but we discover spirit emerging (by a pan-cosmic operation) from Matter."

But these formulas should not mislead us, nor on the other hand should we allow the paradoxical originality of this "spiritual materialism" (or "materialist spiritualism") to lapse into banality. The warning of a circumspect commentator, Paul Grenet, seems to us very opportune: "Teilhard never loves Matter for itself, but only for what comes to fulfillment through it." No more than it should be idolized, should sex be despised or calumniated: it has to be given its rightful place in the service of the masculine-feminine "dialectic." Father Teilhard, faithful to an authentic tradition of Christian thought, admits that the dialectic of man and woman must replace the dialectic of master and slave.

Father Gaston Fessard has developed this theme in his positive critique of Hegelianism and Marxism. "The man-woman dialectic," Father Fessard writes, "is the very form in which the oppositions inherent in the master-slave dialectic can be reconciled." And he proceeds to spell out the conditions under which this dialectic reveals its full richness: "If man and woman unite to give one another, by their very gift of self, a mutual and equal assurance, they can then embrace each other and cooperate in an act which lays the foundation of their unity. Man *possesses*, or rather—according to the biblical expression—*knows* woman as the woman does man, and both are "co-born" to the new being and higher unity which love confers on them even as each takes posession of—and is possessed by—the other.

Man and woman, as Teilhard sees them, are called to a mutual spiritual fecundation: "The man and the woman who are united encounter each other only at the end of their spiritual growth." The Feminine therefore appears more and more as the matrix of evolution, the latter being understood as amorization. For Teilhard,

"Love as well as Thought, is always in the process of growth in the Universe." Each of the spouses must therefore be able to confide to the other what Saint-Exupéry has one of his characters in *Citadelle* say: "Your love is by nature inexhaustible like a source of life. You have become a mediator of love."

Woman, by the power she has to raise up "the love of the invisible," to nourish the impulse "toward all that is beauty and truth," to cultivate "the unlimited possibilities of intuition and of intercommunion will play a crucial part in the progressive spiritualization of love. Whereas Goethe extolled the "Eternal Feminine" who "draws Man upward," Father Teilhard sees the "Universal Feminine" as the "unitive force" thanks to whom the "gradual and grandiose elaboration of a new Cosmos, an Ultra-human sphere, and a pan-Christic Universe can be effected."

IV
Woman Has a Special Mission

Teilhardian optimism, however, never becomes irrational. If this "co-birth" is indeed the
ideal of human love, how many hindrances
there are to the realization of this ideal! Father
Teilhard does not conceal any of them.

First of all, he stresses the risk involved, of
failing to discern the presence of the person
who would bring the desired plenitude, i.e.,
the misfortune that consists in not recognizing
the one who can offer us the "beatifying com-
pletement" we lack: "Against what terrifying
odds," he cries out, "the encounters which make
up the happiness of our lives take place!"

Secondly, assuming that the desired encounter has taken place, how can the contact with
the other be maintained on both levels: that of
exterior activities, and that of interior communication? Teilhard was fully conscious of the
many obstacles to the lasting success of a union

once begun; he denounced "the labyrinths where lovers hear each other without being able to find each other, the impasses where they reach a barren stalemate, the ways that lead them apart, so that through their very union both lose their way."

Finally, are not even the closest and the deepest unions doomed, in this World, to run up against the wall of an ultimate solitude, to meet, eventually, a certain invincible, reciprocal "opacity"?

"Unsuccessful unions, broken unions, incomplete unions"—such is the realistic account Teilhard gives of human love. Woman, as Teilhard sees her, has a major responsibility for the outcome of the couple's perilous adventure. In particular, she is often the source of that "subtle degradation of love" into a deplorable sort of "mutual egoism," which Saint-Exupéry has also stigmatized: "If the woman asks you to be concerned exclusively with her and to shut yourself up completely within her love, she is asking you to share in and abet her own egoism." On woman devolves, to a very great extent, the task of using positively and generously the "affective quantum"—the amorizing energy present in the universe.

In a page from an essay on "the priest," written at the front in 1918 during World War I,

Father Teilhard meditates on the "hesitating and agitated mass," i.e., the reserves of energy accumulated in the Cosmos by "souls led on by various passions: by a passion for Art and the Eternal Feminine, a passion for science and the mastering of the Universe, a passion for freedom and the liberation of mankind." He sees, then, as an intuitive genius, the "fearful crises" caused by the periodic collision of these diversified currents of energy: "they bubble in their effort to equalize themselves." And his meditation concludes with a prayer and a resolve: "What glory for you, my God, what an abundance of life for your Humanity, were all this spiritual power harmonized in you! Lord, I dream of seeing extracted from this wealth—unused or abused—all its inner dynamism. I want to dedicate myself to a collaboration in this work."

To Teilhard, the greatest sin against love is not to offend an often artificial modesty, but to "waste, through negligence or sensuality, the personalizing reserves of the Universe." The gravest danger lives in the sterile closing in upon itself of the loving dyad: either one of the partners becomes a tyrant and stifles even the slightest desire of personal development in the other; or both, giving in to the "sensual temptation to absorption and inertia," run the risk of

losing themselves together "in the enjoyment of
a material possession which would signify for
both of them a regression toward plurality and
a return to nothingness." A misguided longing
for unity thus leads to irremediable division.
Here again, Saint—Exupéry seems to echo Teilhard when he says; "Do not confuse love with
the delirium of possession, which brings the
worst sufferings."

Certainly, "love is an adventurous conquest.
It endures and develops, like the Universe itself,
only by a perpetual discovery. Two people love
each other legitimately when passion leads both
of them, the one through the other, to a higher
possession of their being." On the other hand,
they do not love each other, or rather they love
each other very poorly, who "tend immediately
to shut themselves up in the jealous possession
of their mutual fulfillment" and who are foolish
enough to "limit the promises of the future to
their mutual discovery as if they constituted a
Universe all to themselves." True human love,
on the contrary can only be unlimited openness.
Let us quote Saint-Exupéry once again: "Real
love is a gift, a pure gift, but a gift of each
person to the other, with respect to what he still
has to give."

The specific responsibility of the woman
stems from her twofold and paradoxical power,

in the words of Jean Guitton, "to make man [on the one hand] descend to stupidity and folly and . . . [on the other] to lift him to the heights of excellence through love for her." We meet the same idea in Saint-Exupéry when he says of woman that she can be "the wall I run up against, but also the door that leads to new possibilities," or again, "a step in the ascent toward God." "Woman is the road to heaven," Goethe had already said.

For Teilhard, the "law of growth" is at the heart of everything: the couple—a man and a woman in love—is but a first stage in interpersonal union, and it must "pursue beyond itself the fulfillment that its growth requires." This growth of the couple is possible only if the woman refuses to monopolize her husband's attention and energy for her sole profit and orients them as well toward the growth of suprafamilial communities. "Centration" on self and "decentration" toward others are always mutually complementary in Teilhard's thoughts and the happiness that he praises is born of these two complementary movements: now, the synthesis of these two movements is to be sought in a third which is "super-centration" in a transcendent term: "there is only one way possible for human beings to love each other, and that is to know that both are completely 'supercen-

tered' in a common 'ultra-Center' "—a Center
which is not only "the desire aroused by an Object, but the common attraction exerted by one
and the same Person."

Just as the success of friendship depends on
the friends' interests converging, so too the vic-
tory of human love is assured only if "the Center toward which the two lovers converge by
marriage [manifests] his personality in the very
heart of the circle in which their union would
like to isolate itself." The child, certainly, con-
stitutes a primary object of "supercentration"—
it is evident that the presence of children con-
solidates and fulfills the family. The meaning of
the child, as Father André Marc puts it, is to be
the "immortal fruit of a fleeting act, a living
proof of a love by its nature timeless." Beyond
the child, the "total Center," a guarantee not
only of the perpetuity of the race but of
the survival of the particular personalities of the
spouses as well as of the new soul born of
the conjugal union, can only be God himself, "the
final Term," alone capable of giving true plenitude to love. Those who really love each other
know that it is in him that not only their race
but their personality will be "both saved and
consummated."

In *Comment je vois*, Father Teilhard eluci-
dated the personalist structure of his phenome-

nology with unparalleled vigor: "There is no true love in a collective, i.e., impersonal atmosphere, however warm it may be. Love cannot be born and be stable unless one individual heart, one individual face, encounters another. The more one deepens this essential psychic mechanism of union, the more one is convinced that the only way for the cosmic convergence to succeed, is for it to culminate, not merely in a system of centers, but in nothing more, in nothing less, than a Center of centers." For the positivist Auguste Comte, the mission of women is to be efficacious intermediaries between Humanity and man; for the Christian Teilhard the mediation of the feminine is to foster union between the divine Person and human persons.

Hence, this profound definition of love: "Love is a function with three terms: man, woman, and God." Woman clearly plays a key role in achieving a "harmonious balance of these three elements," since she is called to be *par excellence* the "hyphen" between God and man. On her devolves the task of making man feel that ultimately (in Lacordaire's phrase often repeated by Claudel) "there is only one love," and down deep in all our temporal desires there lives an obscure desire for God himself. But she succeeds in this only by revealing, in the heart of the love she cherishes for her partner, the meaning of sacrifice and of the gift of self: "To attain greater unity within oneself, or to achieve union with others." Teilhard tells us, "one must change oneself, renounce oneself, give oneself: and this process of 'rooting up' is a type of suffering. Each progress in personalization must be paid for: so much suffering for so many unions achieved."

By nature, the woman is psychologically more apt than man to live this relationship between love and the pain that nourishes it. She is also the one whose presence, Guitton writes, "gives sweetness to sacrifice," and very often she is the only one able to inspire man to a renunciation that will enable both of them to grow by raising them together to a higher level. How can we doubt, then, that woman has a special mission, a specific vocation, a unique destiny in the history of mankind?

V
An Anthropology
of Woman

Teilhard never wrote a systematic, differential anthropology but we do find scattered throughout his writings the elements of such an anthropology and illuminating indications of what he considered the challenges specifically facing woman. To begin with, woman is the herald of that fundamental and saving idea according to which there is true freedom only in obedience to one's own vocation. In his *Making of a Mind*, he emphasizes the value of "the present moment" in the perspective of a Christian life: "Believe me," he writes to his cousin, "discard every useless concern for the past and every vague anxiety for the future. Be concerned solely with being obedient to God as you go along, day by day, as he manifests his will to you."

And because woman is more suject than man

to temporal rhythms in her life, she can teach him the meaning and value of time: "In woman," the poet Rainer-Marie Rilke has said, "life remains and dwells in a more immediate, richer, and more intimate way." In Teilhard's view, temporal determinism is the very sign of the creative action of God and the patient acceptance of duration is an assent to rich transformations: "the will of God is in some way materialized or even incarnated in our deepest recesses by *time*, time that sweeps us along and puts rhythm into us, time that passes too quickly or too slowly, time that relentlessly separates from us a long awaited day, or makes the hours of an encounter slip by all too quickly, time that in the twinkling of any eye sets itself against the realized goals we dream of within ourselves and around us, time which ages us."

In 1942, Teilhard advised his friend Claude Rivière to "strive to live the present moment in complete fidelity and in complete awareness," and he gave him his own maxim of life: "Live in communion with becoming, to the extent that every instant of it expresses the totality of God's loving action toward you through the Universe."

To recognize this decisive action of God is to make one's life "passionately interesting even when one is surrounded by inconsequential banalities." It is to understand that "every form of life can be holy," so that "for each person, the ideal form is the one in which our Lord directs him by the natural developments of tastes and the pressure of circumstances."

As Edith Stein (a great Christian philosopher with important insights into the vocation of woman) has observed, woman is, precisely by her specific "essence," "made for the other" and is consequently called to "seize the concrete being in its particularity," with an intuitive vigor which remains uniquely hers. Teilhard, too, sees a major advantage in woman's receptivity, in her tendency to let herself "be modeled." But he sees in it an undeniable danger as well: dissipation (in its root sense) and superficiality. But when woman renounces all futile desires and responds fully and ardently to her vocation, which is to "put herself in the hands of God," she can, through her example, reveal to man all the spiritual benefits of loving sacrifice.

Teilhard may speak rather infrequently of the vocation to bodily motherhood, but allusions to spiritual motherhood abound in his writings—an echo perhaps of that great verse from Isaiah:

Shout for joy, you barren women who bore no children!
Break into cries of joy and gladness, you who were never in labour!

For the sons of the forsaken one are more in
   number
than the sons of the wedded wife, says Yahweh
   (54, 1).

Woman is the being thanks to whom the World
knows a little more of love, and the teaching
profession, to the extent that it requires a "truly
maternal and enlightened" soul, has special
affinities with the feminine genius.

Father Teilhard expected his cousin Marguerite, who was in charge of a pedagogical Insti-
tute, to enhance the lives of those around her by
merging her affection of her students with the
very affection of Christ for them, whereas he
had to admit a certain "masculine inability to
make effective use of sentiment." According to a
remark by Alain, "Woman knows better what
is suitable to the human being and man knows
better what the World needs, the inhuman
World that has no consideration. . . . Man's spirit
is that of the physician; woman's that of the
moralist." Rarely has the beauty of the teaching
profession been better expressed than in those
lines exalting "the philosophic and celestial
grandeur" of teaching, even on a rudimentary
level: "There are very few more effective means
of contributing to the fullness of Christ than
that of forming the souls of children."

Woman's vocation, finally, is to show the way to what Teilhard calls "super-love," because this love is centered on a "super-person." Woman instinctively feels a repugnance for totalitarianism and this repugnance can serve as a timely reminder to convince men that universal convergence and true solidarity will be achieved only as the result of an *attraction* exercised by a freely recognized, transcendent Center. More sensitive than man to the twofold motion which, according to Teilhard, is the moving force of history—the push which comes from above and the pull which comes from below—woman can be the preeminent agent in furthering a universal love in which the "human particles" understand that they "cannot love each other unless they love and fulfill, to some extent, all the others." In this way, woman is seen to be the mainspring of human progress; she bears witness that "what we need is not a tête à tête discussion, nor a hand-to-hand fight, but a heart-to-heart union in love."

Thanks to the profound resources of her psychic nature, the woman is also best fitted to draw attention to the real end pursued by men beyond the pleasures and joys that she herself contributes so generously in giving. The full dignity of woman remains to be attained. Teilhard's thought agrees on this point with that of

Bergson who deplored in *The Two Sources of Morality* the "aphrodisiac" character of our modern civilization and appealed to science for ways to rectify it: "Science has its word to say and will one day say it so clearly that we will have to listen: there will no longer be any pleasure in loving pleasure so much. Woman will hasten the advent of that moment to the extent to which she will truly and sincerely want to become man's equal instead of remaining the instrument that she still is, waiting to vibrate under the bow of the musician. May the transformation take place: our life will be more serious and at the same time more simple. . . . There will be less wastefulness and likewise less envy."

Thus we can say that it belongs particularly to women to show that love always has strength to go on, and that it cannot be exhausted in the trinkets of *well-being:* "It is not a question of well-being," Teilhard cries out, "but of a thirst for *fuller* being which alone of psychological necessity can save the thinking Earth from the *taedium vitae* (distaste for life) under which it labors."

One of the missions of woman is therefore to maintain and renew mankind's zest for life and passion to advance: she is both the one who slakes thirst and the one who excites it, so true is it, Louis Lavelle tells us, that "every being who loves constantly creates about him new centers of initiative, of confidence, of happiness." The woman is the one primarily responsible for this "warming of hearts," which Father Teilhard called in *Les Directions et les Conditions de l'Avenir* (1948), like the "irresistible action" of the forces of convergence and of planetization, the necessary condition whereby Humanity finds itself and forms itself.

Likewise, we may hope woman's increasing participation in public life will play a decisive part in diverting mankind's "great choice" from "the spirit of violence and war" to the spirit of love and "manly gentleness." The choice cannot be avoided and the saving answer can be given only if women have the courage to attest existentially that true strength lies not in aggressiveness but in self-possession, which leads to the gift of self in love. Father Teilhard is one of several modern thinkers who have thrown into relief the importance of feminine values for the equilibrium of humanity: he certainly did not oppose, as clearly as the modern sociologist Bouthoul does, feminine values identified with the desire for happiness, and masculine values identified with the will to power. On the contrary, he argues for a harmonious integration of these two sets of values so that mankind might be preserved from the catastrophes of war. Far

from being that "second sex" which Schopen-
hauer mocked as "always lagging behind,"
woman is more justly regarded as the avant-
garde of humanity on the march toward a mysterious future.

It would be absurd to conclude from this
description of the role he saw as belonging to
women, that Teilhard defended an exaggerated
feminism. In this area, as in so many others on
which he did not hesitate to take a stand, his
attitude was marked by a very careful concern
for moderation. In 1916, he wrote to his cousin:
"A certain emancipation [of woman is] wholly
desirable," but he hastened to add, provided
this emancipation takes place without "mas-
culinizing [her] and especially without taking
away her illuminating and idealizing power
which she exercises simply by her presence and,
as it were, through the very calm of her repose."

The importance of this sort of profound activity has been underscored by Jean Guitton:
"Man's love is modeled after that of woman,
whose silence serves to discipline and enrich
man's impetuous thrust." Father Teilhard also
very keenly felt that woman acts by the very
radiance of her being. The secret of her mission
—in the striking phrase of Gertrud von Le Fort
—lies in "silent, hidden, invisible action," but
if this action is to enjoy any lasting effective-

ness, woman must be truly woman and not that asexual or masculinized being that certain misguided feminists have resolved to raise up. These feminists reacted legitimately, at first, against what really was a "phallocracy," but then soon perverted their reaction into an abstract egalitarianism which was incapable of recognizing an equivalent dignity in the reality of irreducible qualitative differences. Simone Weil has pointed out, with far greater insight than these egalitarians, that "where there is only a difference of nature and not of degree, there is no inequality whatsoever."

Just as Teilhard rejected the attempt to reduce the various races of mankind to sheer identity, and tried instead to foster a mutual respect founded on their *complementarity*, so likewise did he feel that woman should preserve her unique character so that a genuine and fruitful dialogue might take place between the two sexes.

Here, Father Teilhard would certainly have agreed with Nietzsche—the Nietzsche, at any rate, who proclaimed that one must feel in the very depths of his soul what a blessing woman is—when Nietzsche cries out: "Masculinization of women—that is the true name of the 'emancipation' of woman. . . . To me this means a degeneracy in woman's instincts." Teilhard urges a cooperation between the two vocations, masculine and feminine, joining in his customary way a real sense of tradition and a genuine desire for renewal. And so, doubtless recalling the pleasant family atmosphere he knew at Sarcenat, he considers it important "to safeguard by way of rejuvenation" the "old French ideal (certainly somewhat narrow and jealous) according to which the woman exercised a luminous and inspiring influence." This "rejuvenation," characterized by respect for a basic exigence of woman's nature, will be obtained if women, necessarily more accustomed than formerly to the "prose of action," understand the duty which is henceforth theirs, of diffusing the meaning of *evolutionary love*, "of which we may well say that it is the only spiritual energy rich enough in motivating power to make the formidable human agent function perfectly and without danger (either of egoism or of mechanization). And it is in that agent that we find henceforth concentrated, in our field of vision, the entire future and every hope of evolution."

VI
The Physicist's View
of Morality

Teilhard is essentially a moralist. He often stated that the study of the past interested him only to the extent that a better understanding of the past enabled him to better orient and master the future. In a general way, the Teilhardian ethic is a reaction against "a neutral and inoffensive existence." It draws its inspiration from a few simple principles, among which the following are absolutely basic. "All things can be divinized by and through us," and from this certitude there flows "happiness on earth." There is a "true law or natural obligation of carrying on research to the very end. Nothing must remain merely "intended" in the direction of fuller being. "Not only by cosmic enthusiasm but out of *strict natural duty*, one must struggle to *see* clearly, to act more *powerfully*." "We must, under penalty of sin, try all roads"; "we can tend *straight* toward God without turning aside from any truly natural effort."

At the very heart of this bold doctrine one finds the idea that morality is "a direct prolongation of the biological and natural domain." There is, therefore, as Dr. Paul Chauchard has forcefully expressed the Teilhardian doctrine, "a natural, common morality which is the art of using one's head well," for "the normative is imminent to the natural. For the neurophysiologist, egoism is pathological." For Teilhard, just as thought and freedom crown "the psychic awakening of life," so too "does morality fulfill thought and freedom." "The 'moralization' of souls, therefore, prolongs in the most direct way the work of evolution."

In the light of these affirmations we must understand why Teilhard thought that the moralist of our age must be a kind of "engineer of human energy." We indeed see him vigorously oppose the moralist of yesterday, who was primarily concerned with preserving a certain equilibrium between the individual and society, to the moralist of today and of tomorrow, whom he defines as "the technician and engineer of the spiritual energies of the World."

This opposition is linked to the separation

which Teilhard establishes between two types of mind: the "legalists" and the "physicists." The "legalists" are the timid for whom "reality is disturbing as soon as it is found to conceal something more vast and less definable than the artificial (hence easily manipulated) side of our human social relations." For minds like these, "Christ is no more than a king and a proprietor" and mysticism for them is conceived "by way of analogy with a slightly enhanced familial or friendly association." The "physicists," among whom Teilhard places himself, are entirely different. For them, "reality is beautiful only to the extent that it reveals itself as an organic unity." In their eyes, "Christ, sovereignly attractive, must radiate physically" and the truth of Christ is grasped only if we know how to see in him a being who is at once "historical, universal, and ideal."

In this physicist perspective, the Mystical Body of Christ is seen as "the expression of a hyper-physical (super-substantial) relation stronger and consequently more respectful of the individualities incorporated than that acting between the cells of a living organism." Father Teilhard, speaking from painful experience, adds that the "legalists" and the "physicists" will never understand each other and that between the two attitudes in question "we must choose, not by discursive reasoning but because we see." Now, Teilhard saw and he invites us in turn to see what St. Paul had already seen: "The universal and cosmic domination of the incarnate Word," the presence of a "supreme Center of spiritual consistency" in the heart of the Universe (cf. Col. 1, 17).

This, ultimately, is why "the highest Morality is henceforth the one that will best develop the natural phenomenon to its highest limits"—which is identically the spiritual Phenomenon in a perspective of universal ascent of consciousness. Consequently, a morality of ardent movement must be elaborated in the place of a morality of static equilibrium. The future belongs to those who dare to try everything, but not in any way or in any direction for, if Teilhardism exalts the taste for risk, never does it end in gratuitous anarchism or dilettantism. "Try everything and carry everything through to the very end," Teilhard tells us effectively, "*in the direction of the greatest consciousness*," that is to say, in the direction of love insofar as it is "the highest form of human energy." On the contrary, "to limit force," to allow the treasures of human energy to be lost, "that is sin."

This sort of desire for a renewal of morality

has inevitable repercussions on the level of the relationships between man and woman, for it is a matter of "fortifying human love with that incalculable spiritual power that it is capable of developing between spouses." Father Teilhard thinks, as a matter of fact, that we probably still do not have "an exact idea of the functioning and of the best forms of the fundamental complementarity of the sexes." As we continue the search for this "optimum" capable of awakening in man faculties that still slumber in him, a few beacons can even now be lighted in a spirit of fidelity to this imperative which governs the whole process of anthropogenesis: "First think to survive, then live to think." Father Teilhard's central idea here is that humanity must tend toward a profound accord between the sexual sense, the cosmic sense, and the earthly sense. And because woman is more closely linked to cosmic life and more sensitive to its vibrations, she must quite naturally foster such an accord.

The apostles of a love in which man and woman are linked to the entire world in the act which makes them one flesh, had a vague awareness of this truth. Thus D. H. Lawrence wrote: "Marriage is but an illusion unless it is tied to the sun and the earth, to the moon, to the stars and to the planets, to the rhythm of days and the rhythm of the months, to the rhythm of the seasons, of years, of lustrums, of centuries." But how can he fail to see that such a lyrical paganism soon betrays its narrowness and deceptiveness if we do not give it a supernatural dimension?

In the Christian perspective of Teilhard, the cosmic function of love derives its whole meaning from the fact that the Earth is quickened by a movement of spiritualization and of personalization. For Teilhard, to love the Earth is to love the spiritual creature who emerges from it. In a letter of 1937, quoted by Abbé Grenet, Pierre Teilhard reveals an autobiographical secret which is very enlightening in this regard: "The possible meaning of my interior life: the somber purple of Universal Matter changing for me, first into the gold of the Spirit and then into the white incandesence of Personality, then finally into the immaterial (or rather supra-material) ardor of Love."

Envisioning the times to come when the Earth will have reached "the maturation of its Personality," Teilhard can affirm that then, "without ceasing to be physical, love will become more spiritual in order to remain physical. The sexual dimension will be permeated, for men, with the pure feminine." This is possible only because for Teilhard the physical is already meta-physical.

If it is true that "through the love of man and woman, a fiber is woven which extends straight to the Heart of the World," it is important to understand that "it is the Universe that is really advancing through Woman toward Man," a Universe that tends to the spiritual maturation of which it is capable. With the tremor of anguish typical of him, Father Teilhard adds: "The whole question, the vital question for the Earth, is that they recognize each other." Now, it is evident that such a "re-knowing" is possible only if woman is careful to put no obstacle in the way. The absence of this re-knowing means irreparable disorder, the lamentable sludge of the powers of love turned away from their true finality. "Evolutionary" love is love that has become capable of clearly perceiving "the Universal Reality that shines *spiritually* through the Flesh." And a love meant to embrace the All becomes a mere caricature when a man squanders it on an insignificant object.

No one has described better than Teilhard the drama of Don Juan seeking "to rectify the fundamental imbalance in his life by the ever-increasing materiality and multiplicity of his experiences." What is the true character of the woman who is genuinely in love? Teilhard sums up all her nobility when he says: "Woman stands before Man as the attraction and symbol of the World," for woman, however necessary she is as the one who will reflect, reveal, communicate, and personalize the World for man, is not the center of the World." To the new "age of the Earth," characterized by "ethnic saturation" and by "psychical maturation," there must correspond a new form of Love that will find its perfection only in the "complete fulfillment of the Earth," "the terrestrial success of our evolution"—a task which the Creator has willed to entrust to his privileged creature, man.

For man to work toward this distant fulfillment, however, Teilhard felt that he must avail himself of the possibilities opened to him by modern hygiene and biological technology. Since it is a question of promoting a "superior type of humanity," a prudent "eugenics" that will remain respectful of the human person must not be rejected without due consideration. In this very delicate area, once again the Christian Teilhard sweeps away clichés and prejudices and squarely faces problems whose current importance he eloquently proclaims. He denounces the aberration inherent in allowing man "power over all the processes in the World, save those which make him what he is." He likewise affirms the urgent need for courageous reflection on the attempts made by science to "exercise some control over the springs of heredity, the determination of the sexes, and the development of the nervous system," all the while recognizing the exceptionally delicate nature of all these efforts.

To close one's eyes or cross one's arms because these attempts of contemporary biology affect the life given by God is to forget the duty of research which God has imposed on man by endowing him with a thinking intellect: "Precisely because these investigations are delicate and must be pursued rationally, respectfully, and religiously, they require the precautions and the supervision of methodically organized research."

This sort of judgment condemns certain initiatives and experiments which constitute an offense against the dignity of man, but it encourages honest efforts to make better use of "elementary bodily energy." Teilhard does not desire the advent of the "Brave New World"— that best of worlds which Aldous Huxley so famously depicted, but he also rejects a rigid clinging to the past for its own sake, and denounces the snares of a misplaced "piety."

This also explains his attitude toward birth

control and "family planning": there is something absurd, according to Teilhard, in the behavior of a society that "busies itself with everything except organizing the recruitment of its own elements." Questions are being asked today which must be examined in all honesty and without hypocrisy. "What is to be done so that in the numerical optimum of World population all the elements will be as harmonious within and among themselves as possible?" We are at "a dangerous turning point," Teilhard explicitly emphasizes: it is our business to cope with this situation wisely, "aided by Science and sustained by a renewed understanding of the [human] Species."

Who would maintain that woman is not the first to be affected by these problems and that it is not more and more necessary to let her speak out on such subjects? A faithful and penetrating interpreter of Teilhardian thought, Jean Onimus, has observed that a hasty and individualistic use of the techniques of eugenics is undesirable at this time because, as a matter of fact, they alienate man's freedom and responsibility. We agree with him that these techniques will remain harmful "as long as they act mechanically, from the outside, without any positive participation by the people involved, and without a corresponding transformation through love. Instead of bringing freedom, in fact, such techniques would only bestialize, unless they were accompanied by an interior moral evolution which would assure their permeation with human values."

Teilhard himself has shown that, however promising we might find a eugenics that would remain faithful to the Christian ethic of effort and generosity, its promises will have value only through a certain spiritual attitude, which is therefore more important for the couple than all the techniques. This attitude, for which the woman has a very special disposition, is *sublimation* understood as a dynamic power of integration, conserving but transforming all that it transcends: "The World does not divinize itself by suppression but by sublimation." And human love attains its perfection in this effort which leads each of the partners to give up what is best in himself: "When a man loves a woman nobly, with that vigorous passion that exalts the person above himself, the life of that man, his power to create and to feel, his whole Universe, are all clearly seen to be sublimated in the love of that woman." That is why Teilhard thinks that it is time to stop thinking of the relationships between Eros—the love of desire—and

Agape—the love of oblation—in terms of conflict, for these currents of the infinite power of love can join each other and be conjoined with each other "in the evolutionary," in the "genetic"—that is to say, in "sublimation."

The synthesizing thought of Teilhard here finds "an application in a renewed presentation of purity—the Virtue that is so captivating in its mysterious charms and so difficult to interpret!" Rejecting a timid purity of flight and abstention, Father Teilhard sees in genuine purity, "the more or less distinct way in which the ultimate Center of their conincidence makes itself explicit above the two beings who love each other." Thus Teilhard opposes an ethic of separation with an ethic of convergence, but of convergence in God. After having subdued "the winds, the tides, and gravitation," man's self-imposed objective should now be to "subdue the energies of love for God."

Now—and this is one of the points where Teilhard kept his distance regarding the completely "mundane faith" of the Marxist—only a true *super-love* (that is to say, the attraction of a true "super-person") can, of psychological necessity, dominate, subject to its control, and synthesize the host of the other loves on the Earth. Without the existence of such a Center (not metaphorical or virtual, but real) of universal convergence, that is no coherence possible for totalized humanity." Only the recognition of a "Transcendent" makes possible the success of human love and lays open to our vision the legitimate perspectives of a "Universal Love."

Against a superficial view of morality Teilhard defends true *chastity* as an essentially positive virtue which must find its proper place "between marriage (invariably seen by society as wholly directed toward reproduction) and religious perfection (always presented theologically in terms of separation)." The highest chastity then will be "not flight (by repression) but conquest (by sublimation) of the unfathomable spiritual powers still dormant beneath the mutual attraction of the sexes." According to Teilhard, just as certain sensory powers are latent in us and manifest themselves only with a new advance of civilization, so likewise is there an energetic dynamism in love of the spiritual order, the emergence of which awaits a certain "maturation" of the human race.

The men and women who take the vow of chastity because they feel called to this higher form of witness, constitute the extreme point of moral evolution. The triple aim of love, according to Teilhard: "to envelop oneself with the object loved to the point of being inundated by it," "to constantly intensify its presence" and "to lose oneself in it without ever being surfeited with it"—this triple aim is realized, in an even more complete way than in human love, in the relationship which unites the priest to Christ. Even beyond chastity there is maintained and exalted by Teilhard the supreme dignity of *virginity* which supposes a passage to another order and represents a moment of discontinuity relative to the evolutionary continuity of the noosphere: "Virginity rests on Chastity just as Thought does on life."

The virginity lived by souls completely consecrated to God has the value of a sign announcing the new and radiating form that love must take so that some day "the collective passage of mankind to God may be realized"—the passage that, according to Teilhard, marks the end of History. Woman will be the privileged agent of this decisive "transformation of love," because it depends essentially on her that "the call of the divine personal Center be felt strongly enough to overcome the natural attraction." She can make so much noise that this call will not be heard. She can, on the contrary, in the silence and recollection of true love, make this call irresistible. To follow the latter course, however, she must confidently entrust herself to the exemplary influence of the Blessed Virgin Mary.

VII
Mary's Place in
Teilhard's World

Teilhard's entire understanding of woman's vocation is dominated by an attentive meditation on the exemplary person of Mary. Like so many believers whose faith is most virile—such as Péguy and Claudel—Father Teilhard venerated Mary and sought the virtues of which she is the incarnation. If he was able to penetrate so many profound secrets of feminine psychology and to grasp the mysterious part woman is destined to play in the World of tomorrow, it is because devotion to Mary, as Ottilie Mosshamer put it, is "the experience best suited to open to the priest *the metaphysical world of woman:* he who loves the Mother of Christ knows woman."

In Mary, the priest comes to know the substance of femininity as God the creator conceived it, willed it, and loved it." Watching his mother, the young Pierre Teilhard was forever imbued with gratitude and admiring tenderness for woman; later, by turning often to Mary, Teilhard the priest of Christ discovered and honored the ultimate foundations of this reverence for woman which had earlier been imposed on him as a duty.

Teilhard gave a very profound explanation of the Annunciation which he was easily able to tie in with his overall vision of the World: "When the time came and God decided to carry out his Incarnation, he had to raise up beforehand in the World a virtue capable of attracting him to us. He needed a Mother who would give him human birth. What, then, did he do? He created the Virgin Mary; that is to say, he made so great a purity appear on earth that in this transparency he concentrated himself even to the extent of coming as a little Child."

As early as 1916, in a work entitled *La Vie cosmique*, Teilhard had presented the Virgin Mary as "The true Demeter," "Queen and Mother of all things," and he was more explicit when he wrote: "When the day of the Virgin came, the profound and gratuitous finality of the Universe suddenly revealed itself: since the time when the first breath of individualization, passing over the lower, distended Supreme Center, made all the original monads smile in it, everything moved toward the Little One born of the Woman."

We can also understand why Teilhard would have had a very special affection for the feast of the Immaculate Conception: for him it was the feast of "immobile action," of an Action which is supreme because it "is exercised simply by the transmission of the divine energy through us." Now, "to be active in this way and to this degree, the holy Virgin had to receive her being in the very bosom of grace." And it is to the extent that Mary is perfect transparency that she is the model of all women. In her, purity is absolute and purity is the most active of virtues, "because it concentrates God in us and on those who are subject to our influence." Immobile action triumphs in "this one and only luminous activity of drawing, of receiving, and of allowing God to enter." Only insofar as we participate in this Purity, do we become capable of "doing our part in the regeneration of the World."

In her essay on *Woman and her Destiny*, Edith Stein forcefully and in a spirit analogous to that of Pierre Teilhard, brings out the idea that Mary is "the goal of woman's entire formation" and that for woman there is a specific "imitation" of Mary, handmaid of the Lord, as there should be for every human being an "imitation" of the humanity of Jesus Christ. Through the self-effacing imitation of Mary the most efficacious of virtues is propagated: that which transforms souls.

Such a creative imitation is possible only because Mary, as Jean Guitton stresses, has been "more deeply grafted (than Jesus) into our human situation," so that she is forever the auxiliatrix who helps us in "courageously carrying, as she did, a heart full of anxieties." That is why meditation on the Rosary was a prominent feature of Teilhard's spiritual life.

In a letter to his cousin Marguerite Teillard-Chambon, dated October, 1918, he presents the Rosary as "an expanded Ave Maria" and shows that even if the Ave Maria is "at first a particularly instinctive (and often not very disinterested) manifestation of love for our Lady," still this affective manifestation can be transformed into a "need to know our Lady better," to "sympathize" with her. The Heart of the Blessed Virgin somehow becomes transparent and we relive within it "the Mysteries of Christ's life." Eventually, "all doctrine becomes familiar, concrete, and real to us in Mary," and our whole life "is Christianized by the development of the *Ave Maria* in us." Mary is the radiant mediatrix who promotes our union with God and with all things in Jesus Christ.

By giving this preeminent role to Mary and by seeing in Mary the ideal pattern of womanhood, Father Teilhard placed himself squarely in that Catholic tradition which seeks to balance the excessively masculine character of the civilized World. He applauded the "rise of Mariology in contemporary Christianity," attested by the proclamation of the dogma of the Assumption by Pius XII.

Very significant in this regard is Teilhard's disagreement with the Jungian interpretation of the growing interest of theologians in Mary. According to the psychoanalyst, C. G. Jung, the progress of Mariology would be especially the work of women concerned with seeing themselves well represented in the structure of the kingdom of heaven. Teilhard, in defense of the position that "the great votaries of the Virgin have been men: St. Bernard, St. Francis de Sales, St. Aloysius Gonzaga, St. John Berchmans, etc. . . ." replies that "this remarkable rise of Marian devotion alongside devotion to Christ is principally the work of men, especially of men vowed to celibacy." And he stresses in the Marian dimension of Christianity "an irresistible Christian need to 'feminize' a horribly masculinized God (Yahweh)." A better understanding of Mary's importance in Christian dogma leads to a better understanding of God himself, to a "re-discovery" of God in which God is both "cosmized" (brought closer to the universe) and "feminized" in reaction to a certain "neolithic paternalism" too often presented as the definitive essence of the Gospel.

On the other hand, Teilhard was very sympathetic to the notion that God's relationship to creatures is, in its infinitive fullness of perfection, as much "maternal" as "paternal." Surely he would have approved, had he known of it, this cry of love addressed to God by his great friend, Father Auguste Valensin: "Father, he is my Father! How I regret that, because of a mere grammatical convention, I cannot say that he is my Mother . . ." A profound intuition is involved here, and one that succeeds in giving woman an unparalleled dignity.

VIII
The Transcendent
Vocation of Woman

Teilhard held, then, that woman has a transcendent vocation, just as André Breton asserted in his *Arcane* 17. He would certainly have agreed with the surrealist poet that this "vocation, which has been systematically obscured, thwarted or corrupted even down to our own time, will nonetheless be triumphantly reaffirmed one day." But on the other hand, he would have rejected "the notion of a this-wordly salvation through woman." Father Teilhard sought to lead men to a total salvation, both natural and supernatural, and it is by an integral fidelity to Christianity that he helps us to see the decisive role of woman in the quest for this salvation.

According to the most traditional Catholic theology, woman has been created by God from the rib of Adam to be "his helpmate, his likeness, a sort of other self to him." In this World, she is the presence of fertile life, the being who joins force to grace. Through Mary, God's Incarnation in Christ has made the World aware of the grandeur of both spiritual and physical motherhood. Pauline thought has discerned a profound analogy between the natural relationship of man-woman and the supernatural relationship of Christ-Church. Father Teilhard entered spontaneously into this living tradition, bringing together, on the one hand, the data of biology, psychology and sociology; and adding to these sciences, on the other hand, the data of religious Revelation to form a completely perfect, coherent ensemble.

This integral phenomenology not only brings out the meaning of woman's body and soul; it also casts light on God's providential design for her. Looking upon woman as "the attraction and symbol of the World"—of the World in its complete fulfillment—Teilhard can conclude that man, en route toward the ultra-human and awaiting the final transfiguration of the trans-human, "can reach woman only by raising himself up to the stature of the World. And because this World is always greater and always imperfect, and always *ahead of us*, man finds himself involved, in his efforts to win the object of his love, in a limitless conquest of the Universe and of himself." "Man can attain woman only in the consummated universal union," at the end of History when the transfiguring moment of the Parousia will have arrived.

Teilhard's thought thus reveals itself as no less novel than traditional, in that he stresses, more forcefully than anyone before him, woman's responsibility in the awakening of a cosmic sense and in the development of a truly evolutionary love. He refers to the spirit's profound roots in the flesh in a way reminiscent of Péguy's songs in honor of Eve, "the living one." Teilhard read Péguy with admiration, fraternal sympathy, and even, sometimes, with a little envy.

In a letter written to his cousin Marguerite in 1917, he pays homage to Péguy for his "solicitude in defending and praising the 'fleshly cradle' of Christ" and he confesses: "I am slightly displeased with his choice of Eve as his subject. Eve, the 'natural' mother, whose mysterious face is shrouded in the distant past, completely veiled in symbols and legends: what an admirable personification of the necessary and living bonds that indissolubly bind our human race to the evolutionary progress of Nature!" This reminds us to those verses of Péguy in his "Salutation to Eve":

And I love you so much, mother of our mother,
. . . . .
And I love you so much, common ancestress,
. . . . .
And I greet you, O first woman,
Most unhappy and most disappointing,
Most unmoving and most touching of women:
Tressed ancestress, mother of our Lady.

Teilhard also compares Eve and Mary, discerning in them the "two profiles" of woman. The distance between them is not so great and it is very tempting to follow Jean Guitton in his subtle exegesis: "Eva, Ave. Spell Eva backwards and you have Mary's word, the one the angel used to greet her. The change is a minor one, the difference very slight. A smile, a slight lengthening of the lips, and all is changed. Everything changes meaning with Mary (just as everything changes meaning with a smile)."

Yet, if a certain agreement of thought and a certain consonance of lyricism between Teilhard and Péguy are undeniable, there is a thesis of Péguy that Teilhard could not accept. Péguy summarized his pessimistic thesis in this way: "It has never been the lot of any man both to be happy and to achieve his salvation." To Teilhard, the combined enjoyment of happiness and salvation is certainly difficult and rare, but is it not precisely the supreme success of the truly fulfilled woman to know how to reconcile these goods which are so easy to oppose to one another and, by all the means made available to her in view of her particular vocation, to aid the man she loves and the many other souls around him to pursue the hoped-for unity?

Undoubtedly, woman remains essentially "someone on whose forehead is inscribed the word MYSTERY"—as Paul Claudel reminds us in the preface of *Partage de Midi:* "She is the possibility of something unknown, a being secret and charged with meaning. A being secret and unknown to herself." For Father Teilhard, this "secret being" is vested with great responsibilities, rich in beautiful promises, threatened likewise with dangerous temptations, for in this chosen being are joined two sublime vocations, that of Eve, the mother of all the living; and that of Mary, the mother of all believers.